AF231272

WHERE THE RUBBER MEETS THE ROAD
with GOD

Your Moment of Truth

JACK ALAN LEVINE

WHERE THE RUBBER MEETS THE ROAD WITH GOD: COMPANION WORKBOOK
By Jack Alan Levine

Published by Great Hope Publishing, Coconut Creek, FL
www.DontBlowItWithGod.com
www.JackAlanLevine.com
www.GreatHopePublishing.com

Neither the publisher nor the author is engaged in rendering advice or services to the individual reader. Neither the authors nor the publisher shall be liable or responsible for any loss, injury, or damage allegedly arising from any information or suggestion in this book. The opinions expressed in this book represent the personal views of the author and not of the publisher, and are for informational purposes only.

Some of the various stories of people in this book draw from real life experience, at certain points involving a composite of stories. In some instances people's names have been changed in these stories to protect privacy.

ISBN 978-0-9825526-2-9

TABLE OF CONTENTS

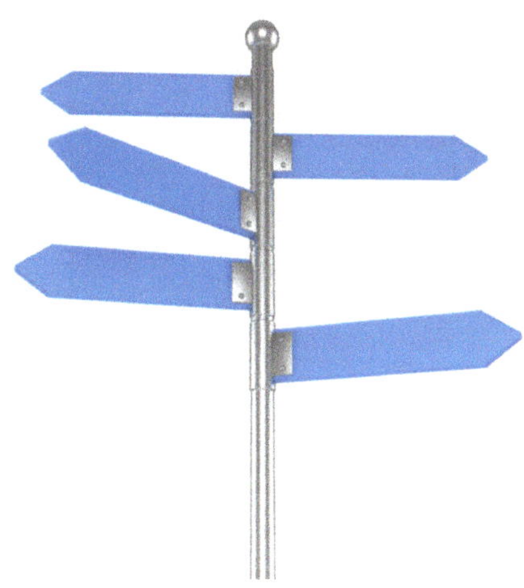

How to Use This Book

This workbook is a companion volume to Jack Alan Levine's *Where the Rubber Meets the Road with God* (abbreviated WTRMTR throughout the volume). Using this curriculum will enable the reader to enhance his or her discipling experience. The disciple will need a Bible (any version) and WTRMTR to benefit from this study.

FOR INDIVIDUAL STUDY

The individual student has it easy. Start at the beginning of each study and keep on going until the end. Simple, right? Each study involves self-reflection (the YOU section), some Bible study (the GOD section), and some interaction with WTRMTR (the WTRMTR section).

INTRODUCTION

This section gives some preliminary orientation for each study and introduces the accompanying chapter in *WTRMTR*.

1. How does the subject at hand affect YOU personally?

2.   What GOD has to say about it in His Word?

3.   How does this appear in daily life (according to *WTRMTR*)?

WHAT DO YOU THINK?

You will answer several personal reflection questions regarding your personal observations about the topic.

WHAT DOES GOD SAY?

You will study some relevant scripture passages and answer questions about them.

WTRMTR: HOW DOES THIS WORK IN REAL LIFE?

This section looks at the applications made by Jack Alan Levine in *Where the Rubber Meets the Road*. You will consider examples and principles presented in the chapter and reflect on the scripture passages.

PUTTING IT ALL TOGETHER

Finally, you will have an opportunity to integrate everything you have learned in the lesson in the last section. The point is to see how everything fits together.

1.   How do I relate to this topic?

2.   What did I learn from God's Word about this topic?

3.   What did I find in WTRMTR that helped me apply God's Word to my situation?

Whether you are studying *WTRMTR* on your own or as part of a group, we trust that God will bless you through these lessons.

> *Whatever things were written before were written for our learning, that we through the patience and comfort of the scriptures might have hope. (Romans 15:4, NKJV)*

> *All Scripture is given by inspiration of God, and is profitable for doctrine, for reproof, for*

correction, for instruction in righteousness, that the man of God may be complete, thoroughly equipped for every good work. (2ⁿᵈ Timothy 3:16-17, NKJV)

FOR GROUP STUDY

MINIMUM REQUIREMENTS

In order to cover the material effectively and expeditiously, two things are required:

1. The leader must do the individual study so he or she is first familiar with it as a student.

2. The group members should do the individual study prior to the meeting so they will each be familiar enough with the subject to discuss it.

WORDS TO THE WISE

Most people have a lot going on in their lives on a weekly basis so your group members will probably have little time to spare. Here are a few tips that may help and bless your study.

---

1. **Defer to the curriculum to carry the lesson along.** The examples and stories from *WTRMTR* are good conversation starters. Those reflections will enable the disciple to see that this topic cannot be academic or theoretical. These emotional issues are where the rubber meets the road with God.

2. **Discern the essentials of the lesson.** If you, as the leader, find it hard to read the material and do the interactions, so will the students. Because of that, after you study the material, you should use discernment to choose which interactive questions, scripture reflections and text interactions are priorities for the lesson. Remember the old saying "Less is more."

3. **Drive the group through the lesson at a leisurely pace, and be willing to take a fruitful detour.** If one question catches the group on fire and they can't stop talking about it, don't shut that down. Make comments based on the other questions you wanted to cover. If they are included in the overall discussion, then can integrate several points into one point- and one point is all any lesson or sermon really needs.

4. **Determine your group's "full" level.** Get a good assessment of your group's capacity for absorbing material. Learn their "tells"; the physical signals they give when they are done listening or talking and ready to move on.

5. **Direct the group away from self-absorption.** Don't let them spend the whole lesson talking about the YOU section. Self-worship is anti-God. This is not a therapy session.

6. **Designate the Bible as the last word on any subject.** Make sure they hear from God. These topics are serious, and humans were never equipped to address these issues without God's revelation. Without clear understanding of God's Word, the group can descend into arrogance swapping ignorance.

7. **Don't do all the talking yourself or tightly control the group.** Do not ask leading questions or closed (yes or no) questions. You shouldn't manipulate the group. You should go to great lengths to make sure the questions are not too easy. Remember God said the Holy Spirit will teach us all things.

1: SEPTEMBER 11—LOVE, NOT FEAR

INTRODUCTION

This lesson addresses something that separates people from God—FEAR. Fear can be paralyzing. This study will seek to understand its effects on our souls as well as what we can do about and with it. What do you fear? What does the Bible say about fear? How does fear affect us in our daily lives?

WHAT DO YOU THINK?

Take a moment to answer these questions:

1. What makes you uncomfortable? List some of those things below.

2. What *terrifies* you? List some of those things below.

3.   What are some things you are completely *unafraid* of that might terrify others?

WHAT DOES GOD SAY?

References to fear appear a total 566 times in the Bible. Fear is a significant Bible topic. Sometimes fear is good—like the fear of God, which is reverent respect. But this chapter focuses on the harmful kinds of fear.

Look at these verses below and write out what they teach about fear. If necessary, be sure to read the verses immediately before and after each of the listed texts to make sure you understand the context of each.

> *For as many as are led by the Spirit of God, these are sons of God. For you did not receive the spirit of bondage again to fear, but you received the Spirit of adoption by whom we cry out, "Abba, Father." (Romans 8:14-15, NKJV)*

> *There is no fear in love; but perfect love casts out fear, because fear involves torment. But he who fears has not been made perfect in love. (1 John 4: 18, NKJV)*

> *And do not fear those who kill the body but cannot kill the soul. But rather fear Him who is able to destroy both soul and body in hell. (Matthew 10:28, NKJV)*

4.   What did you learn from the verses that you did not previously know?

5.   What did you find in the verses that you did not expect?

6.   What did you read in the verses that you did not understand?

WTRMTR: HOW DOES THIS WORK IN REAL LIFE?

When fear is in a person's life, it always affects their mind, their emotions, and their actions. Sometimes that fear is necessary. Fear of stepping out into traffic is certainly reasonable. Proper fear of God actually enhances our worship and devotion, according to the Psalms and Proverbs. Fear can be a blessing or a curse, depending on the object and use of that fear. In this section, we will look at some of the negative effects of fear. This kind of fear does not have God as either its object or its source.

Fear paralyzes

Read the post-9/11 story on pages 1-3.

7. After 9/11, Jack sought a breather by going to a ballgame with his son. Why do you think his son felt it was "the greatest game [he'd] ever been to"? Was it the stress relief, the Dolphins victory, etc.?

Read the pizza paranoia story on pages 3-5.

8. Have you ever been fearful because of a decision or action? Describe the situation.

Fear controls

Read Jack's account of witnessing to his mother on pages 6-7.

9. List some of the people in your life you want to share Christ with but haven't yet.

Read the descriptions of the three friends on pages 7-9.

10. How does fear prevent people from enjoying the blessings they already have?

11. How does fear keep people from accepting Christ?

12. Do you have a familiar habit you engage in when you are stressed or fearful? Is it a positive or negative habit? What usually triggers it? How do you feel afterwards, better or worse? Why? Are you afraid of how you would handle things if you did not resort to this familiar habit or response?

What is my familiar habit?	
Is it positive or negative?	
What triggers it?	
How do I feel afterward?	
Am I afraid without it?	

Fear desensitizes

Read the Jack's story about how God dealt with him concerning two people on pages 12-14, then read Matthew 7:5.

13. How do we reach the place where we decide someone doesn't deserve our love?

Jack writes, "God drew the plank out of my eye so I could see my own despicable sin, so I would realize how conditional my love for others is. He showed me that if I lived in an attitude of humbleness, like my friend Dave when he confessed how far short he was of Christ's perfection, then I would love everybody." (pages 13-14).

14. Has God shown you anything lately? If so, what? If not, what would you like God to show you or clarify for you?

A new commandment I give to you, that you love one another; as I have loved you, that you also love one another. By this all will know that you are my disciples, if you have love for one another. (John 13:34-35)

15. If we are to replace fear with love, what does real love look like?

PUTTING IT ALL TOGETHER

16. In the first section (**YOU**), you considered your own fears. Have you identified how those fears have hindered your acceptance of or devotion to Christ? Explain.

17. In the second section (**GOD**), you read several scriptures about different kinds of fear. Did any of those texts stand out to you as you considered your own fears? Which scripture was most relatable to you and why?

18. In the third section (*WTRMTR*), you saw examples of fear and answered questions about fear that were particularly pertinent to the Christian life. Did you find a story or question that helped you identify the effect your fear has on you or others? Explain.

19. This is where the rubber meets the road with God about fear. What will you do?

Our Father in Heaven, we love You for Your providential care. We thank You that Your angels always preceded their messages by informing the humans receiving them they didn't need to be afraid of good news. We thank You that your Son came to us as the Great Shepherd, the one who leads us through the Valley of the Shadow of Death so we don't even need to fear the great unknown. We thank You that the Holy Spirit You sent to dwell with us and in us fills us with great boldness. We thank You that Your perfect love casts out all fear. Guide us into more courage, more boldness, and more faith in Your loving kindness. Forgive us for fearing things that can't hurt us and for not seeking Your power for victory over the things that can harm us. We give You all the glory and power and honor forever and ever. Amen.

2. FINISHING STRONG

INTRODUCTION

This lesson examines the reasons we fail and seeks to find solutions for our failures. When is failure most likely to occur for a believer? What are the promises regarding failure in God's Word? What can we learn from failure?

WHAT DO YOU THINK?

1. Does *failing* mean you are a *failure?* What does it mean to you?

2. What could you do that God would refuse to forgive when you confessed and repented of it?

3. Have you ever walked away from a situation believing you had failed? How do you feel about it now?

WHAT DOES GOD SAY?

4. Jack used the example of Peter's denial of Jesus to illustrate failure (page 28). What was Jesus' response to Peter's failure?

5. What purpose for Peter might God have had in his failure?

6. Is failure always the result of sin? Is success always the result of righteousness?

7. What should be said to the person who has failed?

Now consider this prayer from David after his sin:

> *Blessed is the one whose sin the LORD does not count against them and in whose spirit is no deceit.*
>
> *When I kept silent, my bones wasted away through my groaning all day long. For day and night your hand was heavy on me; my strength was sapped as in the heat of summer. Then I acknowledged my sin to you and did not cover up my iniquity. I said, "I will confess my transgressions to the LORD." And you forgave the guilt of my sin. (Psalm 32: 3-5)*

8. What prolonged David's sense of failure?

9. List a few of God's promises that we should always remember when we get discouraged or feel like failures as Christians.

WTRMTR: HOW DOES THIS WORK IN REAL LIFE?

The possibility of failure can paralyze a person. Many are terrified of it (see chapter one). To see how commonplace this fear is, do a Google or Amazon search and note the number of books on success. It's not surprising many people today believe that enough prior planning could eliminate failure or at least minimize it.

Failure, though, is in everyone's life—except for those who never attempt anything.

Failure is not final

Read the material about "comebacks" on pages 23-24.

10. Have you ever made a comeback? Describe it.

11. According to Jack on page 23, what makes a comeback possible?

12. What should be our first resort when we fear failure?

13. When you fear failure, do you fall back on the habit we discussed in the last chapter? Does that help you cope, or does it enforce your fear of failure as a self-fulfilling prophecy?

Failure can lead to fulfillment

Refer to 2 Corinthians 12:9 and the material on pages 30-33.

14. What does God continually demonstrate to us?

15. How does knowing the end of a story affect our understanding of it?

16. How does knowing the end of a story affect the effort we put forth (page 31)?

17. When is it too late for a comeback?

Failure must be taken seriously if we are to finish well

Read pages 33-36.

> *But none of these things move me; nor do I count my life dear to myself, so that I may finish my race with joy, and the ministry which I received from the Lord Jesus, to testify to the gospel of the grace of God. (Acts 20:24)*

18. What was Paul's life purpose?

19. Why are our results often second-rate?

20. How does the fact that this life is temporary affect the efforts we put forth?

Failure unaddressed will alter our final destination

Read the story of the father preparing the son to take over the business on pages 36-38.

21. Jack talks about the failure that comes from saying no to God. Is there any place in your life that you're saying no to God?

PUTTING IT ALL TOGETHER

22. In the first section (**YOU**), you considered your own feelings about failure. How has your desire to avoid failure hindered your trust in God?

23. In the second section (**GOD**), you read what the Bible teaches regarding failure. What did you learn from those scriptures? How did they change your perspective on failure and success?

24. In the third section (**WTRMTR**), you saw several examples of failure and answered questions about fearing future failures as well as the value of learning from past failures. Did you find a story or question that helped you identify the effect your attitude toward failure has on you or others? Explain.

25. This is where the rubber meets the road with God about failure. What will you do?

Our Father in Heaven, we thank you that You have never loved us because we behaved well, accomplished a lot, or succeeded in our endeavors. Instead, You chose to love us simply because we were Yours. We needed someone to love us in spite of our sin, and You are the only one who can really do that. We pray that You will guide us through our past so we can utilize the lessons learned from our failures and turn those into wisdom to guide us to future successes. Help us never to discount anything that comes our way because we never know what You plan to teach us. Above all else, Lord, help us to hunger and thirst after righteousness. Thank you for the gift of Your Son, Who made Himself nothing (like us) so we could have everything (You). Please get our attention quickly when we trust something other than You so we will come back immediately to you. Thank You, Father. In Your Son Jesus' Name we pray, Amen.

3. THREE STRIKES, YOU'RE OUT!

INTRODUCTION

This lesson helps us to see the importance of following God's plan no matter what—even if the results are not what we expected or wanted.

WHAT DO YOU THINK?

1. Have you ever been sure you knew what God wanted you to do, only to find out later you were wrong? Write about it.

2. Has there ever been a time you disobeyed God because you thought you'd get better results? Write about it.

3. Has there ever been a time you completely trusted God even though you had no idea how He would or could help you? Write about it.

WHAT DOES GOD SAY?

A man's heart plans his way, but the Lord directs his steps. (Proverbs 16:9, NKJV)

4. What is the relationship between God's plans and our plans?

Now listen, you who say, "Today or tomorrow we will go to this or that city, spend a year there, carry on business and make money." Why, you do not even know what will happen tomorrow. What is your life? You are a mist that appears for a little while and then vanishes. Instead, you ought to say, "If it is the Lord's will, we will live and do this or that." As it is, you boast in your arrogant schemes. All such boasting is evil. (James 4: 13-15)

5. What does James tell us about our plans?

WTRMTR: HOW DOES THIS WORK IN REAL LIFE?

Focus is what determines most of our successes or failures. We need to focus and prioritize our purpose and efforts in our lives. We are constantly encouraged by scripture to keep our focus on Jesus. (Hebrews 12:2, lst Peter 1:13)

Are you looking at the right ball?

Read page 41.

6.　Why don't you know God's perfect plan for your life?

7.　What kinds of problems will you run into when you assume you *do* know God's perfect plan for your life?

Read Jack's story about his nonprofit on pages 45-46.

8.　What did the Holy Spirit point out to Jack when he challenged God about his ministry?

9.　Have you ever had this thought about something you tried to do for God, *"I thought I would accomplish this for You, Lord, and I'm not accomplishing it. Why?"* Describe the instance.

10.　Read Jack's instructions on pages 45 and 46 pertaining to this question. Can you see something you should have done differently in that situation and will do differently next time?

11. According to Jack (bottom of page 45), what is the one bottom-line answer to that question?

Strike One

Read pages 47-51.

12. How can we make sure the Word of the Lord comes to us?

13. Are you following God's exact plan that you already know? Check which of these commands you consistently obey:

I OBEY	COMMAND
	Go and bear fruit that will last.
	Go and make disciples.
	Be the light of the world.
	Love your neighbor as yourself.
	Pray without ceasing.
	Be a servant like Jesus.

14. What did Jack find out about fighting God's will (pages 50-51)?

Strike Two

Read pages 55-58 in WTRMTR and Jonah chapter 3.

15. What did God do for Jonah after he repented?

16. Why isn't it enough to hit bottom? What else do we need?

Strike Three

Read pages 59-66.

17. Why was Jonah angry when God showed mercy on Nineveh?

PUTTING IT ALL TOGETHER

18. In the first section (**YOU**), you considered the way your life reveals what you assume is God's plan. How has your lack of focus on God's actual plan hindered your trust in God? Please explain.

19. In the second section (**GOD**), you saw many prayers, demands, and appeals for God's followers to focus. Most of the scriptures you read concerned paying attention or prioritizing. How has God spoken to you about your priorities as you've studied this lesson?

20. In the third section (*WTRMTR*), you read the story of Jonah, a prophet who didn't want God to forgive him because he believed the people God forgave deserved destruction. We tend to put ourselves in God's judgment seat at times. Has God spoken to you about your self-righteousness (see Job 4:17)? What should you do about that?

21. Following God's plan the way He wants is where the rubber meets the road with Him. Are you focused on things God cares about? If not, what should you do about that?

Our Father in Heaven, we thank You for Your tender mercies that are new every morning. We thank You that You have given us second, third, or five thousandth chance to follow Your plan. Thank You for never giving up on us, in spite of our wandering. We are sheep, constantly going astray, seeking our own way. Thank You for sending Your Son as a shepherd, One who knows who we are and how we are and never stops seeking us. Oh, Lord, help us to never put ourselves in Your place as Judge or Avenger. Lord, help us to remember that we are dust. Lord, help us to submit to Your plan from Your Word, and not to avoid it or look elsewhere. We love You, Lord, but not nearly enough. Our sin is ever before us. Please forgive us and help us to share that forgiveness with everyone we encounter, as Your perfect plan has determined. In Your Son Jesus' Name we pray, Amen.

4. PASS THE SALT

INTRODUCTION

This lesson considers things that contribute to the overall direction we maintain in our lives and the resulting impression this direction makes on others on behalf of Christ. What kind of impression do you make? What is your overall direction? What parts of your life are bland and need some of God's seasoning?

WHAT DO YOU THINK?

1. Consider the past week. Go over your appointments, meetings and interactions with people and review the individual conversations you had. Consider the behavior you displayed. Think about the decisions you made during the week. Now take a step back and assess the whole week. What kind of "taste" did you leave behind?

2. Talk to a few people who know you well and love you enough to tell you the truth. What kind of "flavor" does your attitude have, in their opinion? *Salty? Sweet? Sour? Bitter? Bland? Rotten?*

3. Our attitudes reveal our desires. After your conversation with your friends, pray about your attitudes and
    the desires they reveal in your heart. Do any of these need seasoning? Do any need to be thrown out?

WHAT DOES GOD SAY?

Salt isn't quite as important to us now because of the broad array of seasonings we find in grocery stores and the
refrigeration for our meat. But in Bible times, it was a very big deal.

Salt from the Dead Sea could "lose its saltiness." As the salt dissolved out due to exposure to water or air, the
remaining crystals acquired the alkaline taste of other chemicals and lost their salt flavor and taste. Jesus used
this as a metaphor to illustrate the need for disciples to live lives that were obviously distinctive from the rest of
the world. If a disciple lost his unique qualities, his "saltiness," then he or she was useless (Matthew 5:13; Mark
9:50). Jesus warned his disciples to guard their "salt," their distinctiveness, which was to be a dominant trait of
a believer.

When Christ called His disciples "the salt of the earth" (Matthew 5:13), he was referring to salt's use as a preser-
vative. He assigns His followers the ability to keep things wholesome and worthwhile. Colossians 4:6 reflects
the use of salt as a metaphor for keeping our lifestyles distinctive in holiness.

3. In what ways are you, personally, distinctive for Christ?

4. In what ways are you, personally, lacking where Christ is concerned?

WTRMTR: HOW DOES THIS WORK IN REAL LIFE?

In this study, we are going to look at the *flavor* God wants us to have in our lives (savory, sweet, salty, but most of all, *satisfying*).

The main ingredient

Read the story of The Blind Boys of Alabama on pages 68-69.

5.   What do you think you would do if you had grown up in their circumstances and received the same offer they received?

6.   What was the deal The Blind Boys of Alabama made with God?

Salt curing

Read pages 70-71 in WTRMTR and Matthew 5:13.

7.   How do Christians preserve the world?

8.   Jack realized that he was more interested in the money he could make from some people than he was in their relationships with God. Why were those two things at odds with each other?

Read pages 72-73 in WTRMTR.

9. How can we tell when we are going the wrong way? What little signs should we look for?

10. Answer Jack's question on page 73: What is the current carnival act of temptation in your life today?

Read John 10:10 on page 73.

11. How does Satan tempt us to leave God's path?

Losing saltiness

Read Psalm 40:11-12 on page 79 and continue reading through page 81.

12. Is there anything overwhelming you right now? Describe it.

13. How did Jack restore his saltiness?

14. What is the key to finding God again?

Read pages 82-86.

15. Consider Sam's story. What regrets do you want to avoid?

16. How can you increase the "saltiness" of your life? How can it become more flavorful to God and those around you?

PUTTING IT ALL TOGETHER

17. In the first section (**YOU**), you considered the impression you make on others. What impression do you have of yourself and of the flavor you present to others? Please explain.

18. In the second section (**GOD**), you read material about the theological applications of salt. What are the things God wants your life to be about, according to His word?

19. In the third section (***WTRMTR***), you saw many examples of the effects that Christians are supposed to have on the world around them. Do you see that kind of effect coming from your life? Explain.

20. This is where the rubber meets the road with God about a life of impact. What will you do?

Our Father in Heaven, we praise You for Your ways and how You lead us in them. You have promised Your presence in good times and bad, on the mountaintop and in the Valley of the Shadow of Death, and You are good to Your Word. You have placed in us positions of honor as ambassadors to show the world Your Love. You have placed us in critical positions and charged us with sharing Your Promise with the world around us. You have placed us in priestly positions, responsible for purifying the earth for Your Purpose. We ask not only that You lead us NOT INTO TEMPTATION, but that You lead us TO THE CROSS, lest we forget that there is sin to be saved from. Thank you for Your Ways, Your Calling, and Your Equipping. In Your blessed Son Jesus' Name we pray, Amen.

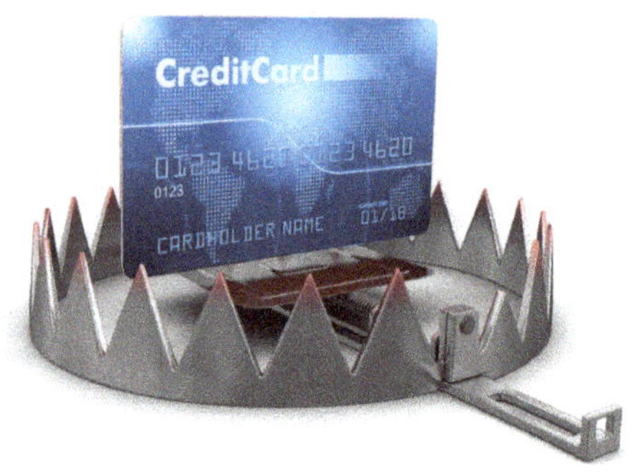

5. THE DEVIL'S CREDIT CARD

INTRODUCTION

This lesson concentrates on the identity we have in Christ, our fight against sin, and risks to our spiritual reputation. How has your spiritual reputation or your "God credit rating" changed since you gave your heart to Christ? What are the conditions for maintaining a good spiritual reputation? What could endanger your new "credit rating" with God?

WHAT DO YOU THINK?

1. Do you believe it's possible for a believer to let his guard down and give Satan access to his spiritual credit line? Why and how?

2. What does it mean to you to have a perfect credit score according to God's rating? And how did you acquire your perfect credit standing before God?

3. Whose responsibility is it to protect our spiritual credit rating and how do we do that?

WHAT DOES GOD SAY?

> *For sin shall not have dominion over you, for you are not under law but under grace.*
> *(Romans 6:14, NKJV)*

4. Jack extensively discussed this verse on pages 89-91. What is meant by "sin" here?

5. What does Paul mean when he says sin shall not have dominion over you?

6. What role does the Law of God play in all of this?

WTRMTR: HOW DOES THIS WORK IN REAL LIFE?

In this study, we will use a financial metaphor (credit rating) to illustrate the importance of *faithfulness* after God has forgiven our sin (our debt).

Spiritual credit rating

In our finances, a reputation for paying our bills on time gives us a good credit rating, which gives us access to more credit. Our spiritual credit rating is based entirely on God's payments.

Read page 88.

8. What is our new spiritual credit rating after we accept God's payment for our sin-debt?

9. What is our spiritual credit limit?

Debt pay-off

Read pages 89 and 90.

10. Will there ever to be a day when sin and temptation will no longer try to ruin your God credit rating while you are on this earth? What can you do to prevent it from being successful?

11. When Romans 6:14 says we are "no longer under law," does that mean that we are no longer held to behavioral standards? If not, what does it mean?

Where credit is due

Read pages 91-94.

12. When you sin, who or what do you *really* blame? Rate these potential culprits in order of occurrence (1, 2, 3...) with 1 being most often.

REASON:	RATING:
MYSELF	
OTHERS	
GOD	
CIRCUMSTANCES	
HEADACHE OR FATIGUE	
STRESS	
MY PERSONALITY	
MY UPBRINGING	

13. Which one of these culprits is usually to blame?

14. Why does it seem easier to blame others than to accept responsibility?

15. Consider this quote from Jack: "A survey from an evangelical Christian company reported that 64% of evangelical Christians do not believe there is a devil." How do you react to that? What do you believe?

Unsolicited credit offers

Read Ezekiel 28:14-15 (beginning on page 91) and continue reading page 94 through page 97.

16. Why did Lucifer rebel against God?

17. Do you ever rebel in similar ways? How?

18. If we've been given God's credit rating, how does Satan get authority in our lives?

Old spending patterns

Read pages 97-100.

19. How does God give us a perfect spiritual credit rating?

Read Colossians 1:9-14 on page 101 and continue reading through page 109.

It does little good to fix your credit rating unless your spending habits change. The Christian life is that way, too. The key to maintaining either type of credit rating is *faithfulness, and/or discipline.* As Christians that means we adopt the lifestyle of grace and live in it fully so we continue to receive all the benefits of a great credit rating.

20. How do we know our sin-debt is paid in full?

Jack quoted Ephesians 6:12-18 on page 103. According to that passage:

21. Why is it so tempting to return to old spiritual spending habits?

22. What guards us against returning to those old habits?

23. Make a list of old spiritual habits you want to give up and new habits you want to start or improve:

#	Give up	#	Start/Improve
1		1	
2		2	
3		3	
4		4	
5		5	
6		6	
7		7	
8		8	
9		9	
10		10	

24. How has Satan been tempting you lately? What can you do about it?

Sin will take you further than you ever wanted to go, sin will keep you longer than you ever wanted to stay, and sin will cost you more than you can ever pay. Faithfulness will keep our spiritual credit rating high.

PUTTING IT ALL TOGETHER

25. In the first section (**YOU**), you considered the importance of a spiritual credit rating. How should the desire to maintain the outstanding credit rating God gave you motivate your actions and the way you live? Please explain.

26. In the second section (**GOD**), you read several scriptures about the things that are trying to ruin your perfect credit rating with God. Do you take Satan more seriously now than you did before this lesson? Which scriptures impacted you and why?

27. In the third section (**WTRMTR**), you saw many examples of the credit-stealing activities that Satan undertakes to destroy your perfect credit standing before God. Did you find a story or question that helped you identify the effect temptation has on you? Explain.

28. This is where the rubber meets the road with God about our spiritual creditworthiness. What will you do?

My Father in Heaven, thank You for paying my sin bill with Your Son's blood. Thank You for raising my spiritual credit rating with Your Son's resurrection. You always take care of me, even when I am arrogant and self-centered and focused on my old destructive habits. I owe You more than I can even imagine. I know I can never repay You, but I can say thank you and be loyal to You. Increase my faith and point me to faithfulness. In Your Son Jesus' Name I pray, Amen.

6. BECAUSE YOU SAID SO

INTRODUCTION

This lesson concentrates on the ability we have in Christ to overcome challenges and sin. When God looks at you, what do you hope He sees? What limits do you place on yourself because of your fallen nature? Are there any areas where you are overconfident?

WHAT DO YOU THINK?

1. What is the most intimidating thing anyone could ever ask of you or challenge you to do?

2. Why does it intimidate you?

3.   What would it take to make you willing to do it?

WHAT DOES GOD SAY?

Meditate on Philippians 3:3-11 NKJV.

> *For we are the circumcision, which worship God in the spirit, and rejoice in Christ Jesus, and have no confidence in the flesh. If anyone else thinks he may have confidence in the flesh, I more so: circumcised the eighth day, of the stock of Israel, of the tribe of Benjamin, a Hebrew of the Hebrews; concerning the law, a Pharisee; concerning zeal, persecuting the church; concerning the righteousness which is in the law, blameless. But what things were gain to me, these I have counted loss for Christ. Yet indeed I also count all things loss for the excellence of the knowledge of Christ Jesus my Lord, for whom I have suffered the loss of all things, and count them as rubbish, that I may gain Christ and be found in Him, not having my own righteousness, which is from the law, but that which is through faith in Christ, the righteousness which is from God by faith; that I may know Him and the power of His resurrection, and the fellowship of His sufferings, being conformed to His death, if, by any means, I may attain to the resurrection from the dead.*

4.   Does Paul recommend that we believe in ourselves?

5.   What is Paul's perspective on his own accomplishments and abilities?

6.   Does Paul mean that our accomplishments or abilities are meaningless? What does he mean?

WTRMTR: HOW DOES THIS WORK IN REAL LIFE?

In the first study, we examined how *fear* can paralyze a person. In the second study we looked at something most people really fear—*failure*. Next, we saw how our *focus* determines most of our failures or successes. In the fourth study, we considered the *flavor* God wants us to have in our lives. In the last study, we looked at the importance of *faithfulness and spiritual creditworthiness*. Now we will consider the kind of *faith* it take to accomplish God's will.

Who believes in you?

In our daily responsibilities, we tend to perform better when we know someone else has confidence in us.

Read the half-pipe story on pages 109-110.

7. What one person could have the greatest influence on you if you knew he or she had confidence in you? Why is that person so influential to you?

8. Why are we so hesitant to trust God in the big things and the little things?

What color is your world?

Read pages 112-118.

9. How have the lenses through which you see the world stopped you from noticing some important things?

Refer to Ephesians 3:17-18 on page 113.

10. How can we gain God's perspective on the world?

11. How can we gain God's perspective on ourselves? Does God think we're *nothing*?

Refer to 1 Corinthians 12:12 on page 117.

12. How does God value team spirit?

13. Does taking orders rub you the wrong way? Why or why not?

Refer to Psalm 51:12, 16, and 17 on page 117.

14. What does *broken and contrite* mean?

Read pages 121-124.

15. Accoroding to Luke 14:15-24 on page 122, what excuses do you keep ready to explain why you don't do as God commands or follow where He leads?

If we refuse to obey God's commands or follow His lead, that means we think we know more about ourselves, our needs, or right and wrong than He does. That kind of attitude always leads to terrible decisions.

16. What didn't Ricky understand about the impact of taking another year to graduate?

17. In what ways have you taken Christ for granted instead of accepting Him by faith?

PUTTING IT ALL TOGETHER

18. In the first section (**YOU**), you reviewed your experience with being intimidated by challenges. Have you identified how those challenges improved your devotion to Christ? Please explain.

19. In the second section (**GOD**), you learned about viewing yourself and your circumstances through God's lenses. What do you need to re-evaluate as a result?

20. In the third section (***WTRMTR***), you saw many examples of people who learned faith and confidence only when they left their comfort zone of *self-sufficiency*. Which story or question most helped you identify the effect your fear has on you or others? Why?

21. This is where the rubber meets the road with God about faith. What will you do?

My Father, You have already done everything for me, but You insist I have a right to even more. Sometimes I don't know what to make of that, and I have a difficult time accepting what You have for me. I have a really hard time obeying Your commands when I think I have a right to do whatever I want. I have an even more difficult time following You when I don't know the destination or how long it will take to arrive. The fact is that I have a hard time trusting anyone, Lord, and I have a hard time trusting You, too. I'm sorry for that. Help me put that away so I can live in the confidence that only comes from You because You've already done everything for me. Thank you. In Your Son Jesus' Name I pray, Amen.

7. PAIN, PAIN, GO AWAY

INTRODUCTION

This lesson concentrates on the choice we have to live lives of thankfulness or follow the selfish and self-pitying way of the world.

WHAT DO YOU THINK?

A "funk" is a state of paralyzing fear or a depressed state of mind.[1] When you are in a funk, you can sound a little like the author of Ecclesiastes who basically said "I hate life. As far as I can see, what happens on earth is meaningless."

1. When we are hurt or disappointed, why do we complain first? What is God's cure for a "funk" or depression? What should we look for as we work through our funk or depression?

2. Think back on the last time you went through real pain (emotional, financial, physical, whatever). Write a paragraph describing the circumstances of that pain.

---

1   http://www.merriam-webster.com/dictionary/funk

3. What do you remember most about that pain?

4. Did anything positive come out of that pain? If so, what was it, and why was it positive?

WHAT DOES GOD SAY?

Everyone hates pain. But attempting to always avoid or numb pain can lead us into disaster.

5. In Colossians 2:6-7 (page 126) and 1 Thessalonians 5:16-18 (page 127), when are we supposed to be thankful?

6. In Luke 21:34 (page 128), Jesus talks about drunkenness, anxiety and dissipation (excess indulgence). How can dissipation cause us to miss out on God's best for our lives?

7. It's hard to give thanks when we are in pain. What is the role of focus in understanding the reason for our pain and trusting God through it (pages 131-132)?

Therefore, in order to keep me from becoming conceited, I was given a thorn in my flesh, a messenger of Satan, to torment me. Three times I pleaded with the Lord to take it away from me. But he said to me, "My grace is sufficient for you, for my power is made perfect in weakness." Therefore I will boast all the more gladly about my weaknesses, so that Christ's power may rest on me. That is why, for Christ's sake, I delight in weaknesses, in insults, in hardships, in persecutions, in difficulties. For when I am weak, then I am strong. (2 Corinthians 12:7-10, NIV)

8. Why did Paul believe his pain came to him?

9. Who allowed his pain?

10. What consoled him in his pain?

11. What do you think of this phrase: "When I am weak, then I am strong"?

WTRMTR: HOW DOES THIS WORK IN REAL LIFE?

In this lesson, we look at one of the challenges to our faithfulness and the *funk* we are prone to fall into when we face spiritual, emotional, financial, or physical pain.

Read pages 125-127.

12. Why would a thankful attitude make recovery from drug addiction easier?

13. How is gratitude a counterbalance to depression?

14. React to Jack's statement "my sciatica was killing me and I was grateful?" Do you respond the same way to trials and tribulations in your life? Give an example.

15. How is it possible to simply *be joyful* in all circumstances?

Your attention target determines your attitude

Read Jack's story on pages 127-129.

16. What is your major life anxiety?

17. How has your pain shaped your behavior and attitudes about life?

18. How has your pain affected the way you behave towards and treat other people?

Read Luke 9:62 on page 129 and Luke 21:34 on page 130.

19. What parts of your past should you avoid dwelling on?

20. What parts of your past should you never forget?

Read pages 137-139.

The scriptures, stories, quotations, and teachings we've read in Jack's book and this workbook bring us to a final solution—*thankfulness* as a counterbalance to *funks*. Both of these have far-reaching results. Funks increase your negativity and decrease your effectiveness, reduce and hurt your relationships, and kill your spirit. On the other hand, thankfulness over forgiveness for sin and for God's presence throughout your pain produces something wonderful.

21. What does thankfulness help you produce?

22. What is the prerequisite for being a disciple?

23. What is Christ's ultimate plan for us?

PUTTING IT ALL TOGETHER

24. In the first section (**YOU**), you considered your own experience with painful circumstances. Have you been able to identify how those funks hindered your acceptance of or devotion to Christ? Please explain.

25. In the second section (**GOD**), you read several scriptures about the importance of being thankful. Which scripture was most relatable to you and why?

26. In the third section (*WTRMTR*), you answered many questions that were particularly important to living the Christian life. Did you find a story or question that helped you identify the effect your funk or depression has on you or others? Explain.

27. Who is in the driver's seat with your emotions? Your circumstances or your thankfulness?

Thankfulness is where the rubber meets the road with God.

My Father in Heaven, I have an enemy who does everything he can to make me feel sorry for myself. He piles up circumstances so high that I can't see over them and I am terrified that I'm surrounded. But I know he was Your enemy first, and You can easily see past all the circumstances to find me and lift me up. Lord, open my eyes that I might see all the good things You've already done. Help me not to be the kind of person who thinks I can manipulate You into blessing me because I'm good. You designed me to be the kind of person who is good because I have been blessed. I love you Lord, and never let me forget Who was there for me when sin ruled my life. Thank You for being that One Who sticks closer than any brother. In Your Son Jesus' Name I pray, Amen.

8. YOU BE THE JUDGE

INTRODUCTION

This lesson concentrates on the gradual changes God wants to make in us as we continue our spiritual journey with Him.

1. How do we know when God is trying to change us? How much maturity is enough? Is God ever satisfied with our progress?

WHAT DO YOU THINK?

2. Have you ever missed out on something because you quit too early? What was it?

3. Who are some of your role models? How well did you do when you modeled yourself after them?

4. Use the scale below to rate yourself in different areas of maturity. Circle the ones that best describe you.

PHYSICALLY

| WEAK | UNDER-DEVELOPED | EXCELLENT | OVER-WEIGHT | EXHAUSTED |

EMOTIONALLY

| UNCONTROLLED | CHILDISH | BALANCED | STIFF | COLD |

SPIRITUALLY

| LACKING | WEAK | HUMBLE | PROUD | ARROGANT |

WHAT DOES GOD SAY?

*Do not be conformed to this world, but be transformed by the renewing of your mind, that you may prove what is that good and acceptable and **perfect** will of God., (Romans 12:2, NKJV)*

5. How much influence would you say God has in your thinking?

Do you not know that in a race all the runners run, but only one gets the prize? Run in such a way as to get the prize. Everyone who competes in the games goes into strict training. They do it to get a crown that will not last, but we do it to get a crown that will last forever. Therefore I do not run like someone running aimlessly; I do not fight like a boxer beating the air. No, I strike a blow to my body and make it my slave so that after I have preached to others, I myself will not be disqualified for the prize. (1 Corinthians 9:24-27, NIV)

6. What do you think is the prize Paul was running for?

7. How do you think your pastor feels about believers who will not mature?

8. How do you think God feels about them?

WTRMTR: HOW DOES THIS WORK IN REAL LIFE?

In this study, we look at how God *fine-tunes* us to make us more like Jesus. This is probably the most important need Christianity faces at this time. Yet many professing Christians in the United States are *junk food* disciples. We like our religion hot, fast, and convenient. We do not like to spend time or effort on it. When we go to church, we expect a flawless, easy-to-digest presentation. We do not want to think too much.

The problem with that kind of Christianity is that any kind of true, positive development that has staying power usually requires real time and effort. You cannot just become Christ-like when it's convenient. It is a moment-by-moment, developed and practiced spiritual way of life. Like a physical exercise or health regimen, one that must be implemented, strengthened and maintained daily in order to have long lasting results and benefits.

The reason I've called you here today...

Read pages 159-161.

9. What was God's agenda for Jack's divine appointment?

10. Have you ever realized that a divine appointment had been scheduled for you? What was it?

Jack discussed a sermon he heard from John 13:12-17. Read that passage in your Bible.

10. How does serving others demand maturity?

11. Are you living a life of sacrifice and service to God? Can you prove it? How?

Read the discussion of John 15:10 on pages 161-162.

12. Why should we live a life of sacrifice?

13. How is self-sacrifice beneficial to us as well?

14. What does disobedience cost?

Proof of life

15. Complete the statements below by filling in your name, but only next to the statements that if we were describing you would be true.

MY NAME	LOVING ACTS[1]
	is always patient
	is always kind
	never envies
	never boasts
	is never arrogant
	is never rude
	never insists on his/her own way
	is never irritable
	is never resentful
	never rejoices about wrongdoing
	always rejoices with the truth
	tolerates everything life brings
	believes everything God says
	hopes in everything God says
	endures every trial he/she faces
	never gives up
	speaks maturely
	thinks maturely
	reasons maturely
	gave up childish ways

There's no such thing as "just" a sin.

Read pages 164-172, which includes 1 Corinthians 2:6, 15; 9:24-27; 11:31.

16. Complete the following statement: *God has shown me where I fall short in order to make me a better servant and that means fixing:*

17. Here is an important thought—God expects you to manage yourself. He expects you to evaluate yourself in terms of Christian maturity. Have you ever done that? If not, when will you do it?

PUTTING IT ALL TOGETHER

18. In the first section (**YOU**), you reviewed your own maturity level. How do you think you're doing? Please explain.

19. In the second section (**GOD**), you read several scriptures about the ways spiritual maturity manifests itself in our lives. Did any of those texts have particular importance with you as you considered your own maturity? Which scripture was most relatable to you and why?

20. In the third section (***WTRMTR***), you saw many examples of maturing. Did you find a story or question that helped you identify the effect God's efforts have had in maturing you in your life? Explain.

21. Have you given sin a vote in your life and decision-making process? *Because that's where the rubber meets the road in maturity.*

Bow your head right now and ask God to show you which of the empty blanks on the list in question 14 demands your immediate attention. Fill in the blank on this statement with your name and date the statement—if you mean it.

Dear Lord, You have revealed a major problem of immaturity. I need to fix it now.

I ask You to show me from Your Word what my next step should be.

I will obey Your direction. I will seek Godly counsel.

Please place a godly mentor/discipler in my life who I can learn from first hand.

I will follow their directions from Your Word.

I want to become the discipler You desire me to be.

Please make me aware of the fine-tuning You are doing in my heart.

Please compel me to keep on following Your direction

so that I can fit the definition of love in Your Word, as Your Son did.

My Signature									Date

9. WHO SAYS YOU HAVEN'T GOT A PRAYER?

INTRODUCTION

This lesson surveys the basic truths of prayer.

WHAT DO YOU THINK?

Do you agree with saying "To be a Christian without prayer is no more possible than to be alive without breathing."

1. How do we know God will listen to us when we pray? Why does God listen to us? What are some of the rules for prayer?

2. Rate your prayer life: (1 being the best, 10 being the worst)

    - *Regularity* denotes how often you pray.

    - *Length* denotes how long you pray.

    - *Passion* denotes how serious you are in your prayers.

- *Perseverance* denotes how long you stick with a prayer request.

- *Worship* denotes your reverence for God ("Our Father which art in heaven, hallowed be Thy Name…")

- *Submission* denotes your obedience to God's plan ("Thy Kingdom come. Thy will be done on earth as it is in heaven.")

- *Requests* denotes your dependence on God for your needs ("Give us this day our daily bread.")

- *Confession* denotes your recognition of your own sin and forgiveness of offenses ("Forgive us our debts as we forgive our debtors.")

- *Sanctification* denotes our desire to be holy people ("Lead us not into temptation, but deliver us from evil.")

- *God's Authority* denotes whom you depend on for everything ("For Thine is the Kingdom and the power and the glory forever. Amen.")

Quality	Poor		Mediocre		Average		Good		Great		Sub-totals
Regularity	1	2	3	4	5	6	7	8	9	10	= ______
Length	1	2	3	4	5	6	7	8	9	10	= + ______
Passion	1	2	3	4	5	6	7	8	9	10	= + ______
Perseverance	1	2	3	4	5	6	7	8	9	10	= + ______
Worship	1	2	3	4	5	6	7	8	9	10	= + ______
Submission	1	2	3	4	5	6	7	8	9	10	= + ______
Requests	1	2	3	4	5	6	7	8	9	10	= + ______
Confession	1	2	3	4	5	6	7	8	9	10	= + ______
Sanctification	1	2	3	4	5	6	7	8	9	10	= + ______
God's Authority	1	2	3	4	5	6	7	8	9	10	= + ______
									Total		

Scores   1-20 *Poor*   21-40 *Mediocre*   41-60 *Average*   61-80 *Good*   81-100 *Great*

3.   Most Christians feel inadequate in their prayer lives. Where do you feel you're falling short?

WHAT DOES GOD SAY?

Prayer is the "addressing and petitioning of God."[1] A classic definition of Christian prayer is "an offering up of our desires unto God, for things agreeable to His will, in the name of Christ, with confession of our sins, and thankful acknowledgement of His mercies."[2]

4.   When we are disobedient, what kinds of answers can we expect to our prayers?

5.   Do you let your prayers be deeply personal, or are they somewhat routine and automatic? Do they concentrate mostly on physical needs or spiritual issues?

On page 185, Jack encouraged you to read Acts 12. Read it and answer:

6.   What does this chapter tell you about the sovereign plan of God?

7.   How is God's sovereignty an *encouragement* to pray?

---

1   Baker Encyclopedia of the Bible, Elwell & Beitzel, 1745.

2   Baker Encyclopedia of the Bible, Elwell & Beitzel, B. J. 1745.

WTRMTR: HOW DOES THIS WORK IN REAL LIFE?

In this study, we consider the *favor* God shows us every moment through the gift of prayer.

Life is hard

Read Jack's story on pages 173-177.

8.   Why did Jack's perspective change when he learned that Kathy was praying for him?

9.   How does it bless us to pray for others?

10. Since giving his life completely to God, what does Jack understand his purpose for living to be?

Read pages 178-180.

11. Have you ever been put to the test in a severe way and come out "refined"? Describe that experience and what was different about you when you finished?

12. How did the people in Hebrews 11 manage to prevail? What does that have to do with prayer?

13. Explain why it is easier or harder to praise God when things are going well? Explain why it's easier or harder to depend on God when things are going well?

Read pages 181-192.

The rest of this section will be an application of Jack's lessons to your personal life. If you've never had experience with a particular prayer lesson he learned, just write "none" in that blank. However, if you have had experience, briefly jot down what you learned from that lesson in prayer.

Prayer Lesson	My experience with this lesson
1 **When God puts someone on your heart, you need to pray for them.** (Hebrews4:7, James 1:22).	
2 **Prayer works.** (2 Kings 18:5; 20:1; Jeremiah 11-13; Genesis 18:16-19:29; Luke 16:10)	
3 **Prayer is about getting us into God's mindset, not the other way around.** (Hebrews 12:2, Luke 22:42)	
4 **God will say no to a prayer that is not aligned with His will.** (I John 5:14)	
5 **God will say yes to a prayer that is aligned with His will.** (John 14:13-14; 15:16; 16:24.	
6 **Our prayers' effectiveness depends on our relationship with God.** (James 5:16)	

Prayer is for regular people. **7** (James 5:17-18).	
Prayer is a weapon against our enemy. **8** (Ephesians 6:18)	
We should always pray. **9** (1 Thessalonians 5:17)	
Jesus Himself prays for us. **10** (Romans 8:34, Hebrews 9:24, Romans 8:26)	

PUTTING IT ALL TOGETHER

14. In the first section **(YOU),** you reviewed your own prayer life. Have you identified weaknesses in your prayer life? Please explain.

15. In the second section **(GOD),** you looked at some scriptures specifically addressing prayer. Did God use any of those verses to speak to you as you considered your own prayer life? Which scripture was most relatable to you and why?

16. In the third section **(WTRMTR),** you read Kathy's story and had the opportunity to review your prayer experience. Are you happy with your experience? Explain.

Read the prayer on page 193.

17. Here's where the rubber meets the road with prayer. Using the prayer lessons listed above, in your own words write a prayer about your prayer life:

____

____

____

____

____

____

____

____

____

____

____

____

In Jesus' Name I pray, Amen.

10. IT HAPPENED TO ME

INTRODUCTION

This lesson considers our attitude toward things like backsliding, cheating, giving in to sin and lack of commitment. We will cover issues like these: Why do we wander away from God? Who is to blame? How can we cast out sin?

1. Think about something you did that God forbade. Why did you do it?

2. How did you feel about it immediately afterwards?

3. How do you feel about it now?

4.   Have you ever tried to stop someone from acting on a bad decision? How did it go?

WHAT DOES GOD SAY?

Read Jack's discussion of Psalm 106 on page 196 and of James 1:13-16 on page 198.

5.   How does sin creep up on people who know God?

6.   Where does the temptation to sin come from? Who is responsible for it?

7.   When are we often most vulnerable to sin?

WTRMTR: HOW DOES THIS WORK IN REAL LIFE?

In the first study, we examined how *fear* can paralyze a person. In the second study we looked at something most people really fear—*failure*. Next, we saw how our *focus* determines most of our failures or successes. In the fourth study, we considered the *flavor* God wants us to have in our lives. Then we examined the importance of *faithfulness* after God has forgiven our sin-debt. We considered *faith* in God and in ourselves. After that, we looked at one of the challenges to our faithfulness—the *funk* we are prone to fall into when we face spiritual, emotional, financial or physical pain. After that, we saw how God *fine-tunes* us to make us more like Jesus. In the last chapter we looked at the *favor* God shows us every single moment through the gift of prayer. Now we're going to consider the importance of *forsaking*, casting sin from our thoughts, emotions, and actions.

Are God's Words empty?

Read pages 195-196 and Isaiah 55:11; Hebrews 4:12-14 on page 195.

8. Is God's Word supposed to make a difference?

9. Make a list of some old habits and characteristics that are supposed to be gone since you accepted Christ, and your explanation for holding on to them.

	My Old Trash List	Explanation for Holding On
1		
2		
3		
4		
5		
6		
7		
8		
9		
10		

Read Isaiah 59:1-2 and Psalm 106 on page 196.

10. Go over that list you made and circle the number(s) of the item(s) that are obviously hindering your relationship with God right now.

11. Has God dealt with you about those things before? Why are they back?

The blame game

Read pages 197-199, John 6:63 on page 197 and James 1:13 on page 198.

12. When God starts bugging us about our behavior, what does that prove?

13. What is God's tool for giving us life?

Read Jack's account of how God dealt with him and his sin on page 198.

14. What is standing between you and God right now? Why do you think you can't you get past it?

15. Why does God want our sins brought to Him?

16. What sin-habits do you attribute to your upbringing, temperament, and genetic makeup?

How God thinks

Read pages 199-200

17. What did Jack finally figure out about the source of his sin?

18. How can God's love deal with our sin?

19. If God knows all your thoughts anyway, why do you have to come clean with Him?

This way out

Read pages 200-204.

20. Explain why we shouldn't be arrogant about our ability to stand up to sin.

PUTTING IT ALL TOGETHER

21. In the first section (**YOU**), you reviewed your history of disobeying God. How did you feel about yourself after answering those questions? Please explain.

22. In the second section (**GOD**), you read several scriptures about how sin works. Which of those texts spoke to you the most as you considered your own history?

23. In the third section (**_WTRMTR_**), you considered a lot of things that you _ought_ to quit. What's your plan for doing that? Explain.

24. This is where the rubber meets the road with God about sin. What will you do?

My Father in Heaven, I quit. At least I want to. All that stuff I said couldn't be helped; all the times I explained my behavior away and said, "Take it or leave it;" all the times I gave in to my old nature—I need those things out of my life. Your Son died for me, so I know the price for my sin has been paid. You created me in Your image, so I know You've equipped me to pursue holiness. Your Spirit abides in me, so I know I'm not left on my own You have done Your part Lord. You have kept every promise. So now I call upon You to do the thing Your Son commanded me to pray for—"Lead me not into temptation, but deliver me from evil." I humble myself, pray, seek Your face, confess my sin, and turn from my evil ways. Cleanse me and sanctify me for Your service. In Your Son Jesus' blessed Name, and on the authority of Your Own promises, Amen.

11. STRUGGLES WITH SIN

INTRODUCTION

This lesson takes a look at the battles we face with self and Satan. Why can't we get past temptation once and for all? What is our daily strategy for addressing temptation? How much of resisting temptation is me, and how much is God?

WHAT DO YOU THINK?

Once we have received our citizenship in the Kingdom of Heaven, we often face spiritual warfare. Living the Christian life will certainly bring its share of struggles. God wants us to fight as warriors so that the way we fight against the *enemy* is often the factor that sanctifies or condemns a fight.

1. Think back on your experiences in junior high school, high school or college. Did you have an enemy? Who was it?

2. What did that person do that made them your enemy?

3. Much of the chapter deals with selfish ambition. Have you ever let what you wanted in life push other people out of the way? Did it push God out of the way?

WHAT DOES GOD SAY?

Spiritual warfare is a popular subject. Many teachers are spreading many things about the subject—things that sound pretty exciting and exotic. We should be discerning when we read these. The painfully dangerous and powerful thing about sin, temptation, and satanic assault is not its mystery, but its commonality, its *normalcy*. It's everywhere you go, and it looks like a pretty girl, a handsome man, a great job offer, a fun party, or a one-time opportunity to make money. Satan doesn't operate in pagan temples or drug empires nearly as often as he resides in convenience stores, suburban living rooms, office complexes, and school hallways. The Bible has quite a lot to say about struggles.

Read James 1:19-21 on page 208.

4. How can impulsiveness get us in trouble?

5. Just trying to "do better" is not enough. What else is needed?

WTRMTR: HOW DOES THIS WORK IN REAL LIFE?

Most human beings have emotions or moods that increase or decrease depending on stress, lack of stress, weather, sickness, health, hunger, plenty, weariness, idleness, mistreatment, or luxury. We humans are quirky in that our moods often do not match our circumstances.

Circumstantial Wisdom

Read Jack's story on pages 205-208.

6.   React to this statement: "Restlessness crept in."

7.   What does a "nudge" from God feel like?

8.   Can you think of something you wanted and convinced yourself it was God's idea? Describe it and its consequences.

Advice from Jesus' younger brother

Read James 1:19-21 on page 208.

9.   How does *listening* help us in our struggle with sin?

10. How can anger be slowed down?

Read James 3:13-18 on page 209.

11. What seems to be the opposite of bitter envy and selfish ambition?

12. What do our good deeds show?

13. What is wisdom?

14. Why do we need wisdom?

15. Where do we begin our search for wisdom?

16. How are bitterness and envy "gateway sins" to worse things?

Read 1 Timothy 6:6-12.

17. What did God reveal to Jack from that scripture?

18. How does seeing the world as "temporary" help us resist sin?

19. Why do people follow money more than God?

20. How can the desire for money separate us from Gods plan for our life?

21. What is contentment?

Read 1 Timothy 6:6-12.

PUTTING IT ALL TOGETHER

22. In the first section (**YOU**), you reviewed your history of conflict. Have you been able to identify how those conflicts have hindered your acceptance of or devotion to Christ? Please explain.

23. In the second section (**GOD**), you saw that God's word tells us that we must fight sin and Satan. Did any of those scriptures stand out to you personally as you considered your own struggles with sin? Which scripture was most relatable to you and why?

24. In the third section (*WTRMTR*), you saw James' advice for struggling with sin. Did you find a scripture that changed your perspective on temptation and spiritual warfare? Explain.

25. This is where the rubber meets the road with God about struggling with sin. What will you do?

My Father in Heaven, I see through Your Word that I am called to be a soldier in Your army, commissioned to do battle with sin and Satan. Help me to choose and utilize all Your weapons. Help me to live a life focused on the Spirit and not on my flesh. Help me to depend on the Sword of the Spirit, which is the Word of God. Give me Your perspective on this battle so that I know I am surrounded by Your angels, who fight the battle I cannot see. Give me the faith to fight the good fight. Thank You, Lord, for the victory. In Your Son Jesus' Name I pray, Amen.

12. ARE YOU READY?

INTRODUCTION

This lesson considers our eternal destiny that God has offered through salvation and the rewards that come with it. What will we do with our lives? What can we expect during our lives? What is "eternal life"?

WHAT DO YOU THINK?

Ask yourself these questions to prepare for this lesson:

1. If you died right now, where would you spend eternity?

2. What does "eternal life" mean to you?

3. Do you believe in heaven? Why?

4.   What is the purpose of heaven?

5.   Do you believe in hell? Why?

6.   What is the purpose of hell?

WHAT DOES GOD SAY?

Eternal life has a much bigger emphasis in the New Testament than in the Old Testament. In fact, the first time "eternal life" is mentioned in the Bible is in Matthew 19:16-22 and its parallel passages in Mark 10:17-27 and Luke 18:18-27. The first person to ever describe eternal life was Jesus Christ Himself.

7.   What kinds of things block people from receiving eternal life?

Eternal life is the result of believing on Jesus Christ as Savior.

> *As Moses lifted up the serpent in the wilderness, even so must the Son of Man be lifted up, that whoever believes in Him should not perish but have eternal life. For God so loved the world that He gave His only begotten Son, that whoever believes in Him should not perish but have everlasting life. For God did not send His Son into the world to condemn the world, but that the world through Him might be saved. (John 3:14-17, NKJV)*

8.   As you stand with God right now, do you have a right to eternal life? If not, what should you do about that? If so, what has been the key to your good standing with God?

Eternal life was defined by Jesus.

He explained eternal life at the Last Supper during His High Priestly Prayer: *"This is eternal life, that they may know You, the only true God, and Jesus Christ whom You have sent."* Here is the definition of eternal life, from John 17: 3, directly from Jesus: *Eternal life is knowing God. When you know God you can be certain of God's provision for you in this life and for all eternity.*

9.   How do you think a non-Christians definition of eternal life matches up with Christ's definition?

Eternal life is a present possession.

That means we do not have to wait until we die to have eternal life. We aren't dealing with "spiritual escrow." We have our inheritance now. John wrote:

> *God has given us eternal life, and this life is in His Son. He who has the Son has life; he who does not have the Son of God does not have life. These things I have written to you who believe in the name of the Son of God, that you may know that you have eternal life, and that you may continue to believe in the name of the Son of God. (1 John 5:11–13)*

10. How does seeing eternal life as a "here and now" issue as well as a "there and then" promise affect a believer's perspective?

Receiving eternal life is a conditional arrangement.

We get it by being saved from our sins. *"For the wages of sin is death, but the gift of God is eternal life in Christ Jesus our Lord." (Romans 6:23)*

11. What is the condition for receiving eternal life?

WTRMTR: HOW DOES THIS WORK IN REAL LIFE?

What do you do with the dash?

Read pages 215-217.

12. How old are you? Are you happy with what you have accomplished in your life so far?

Read Psalm 39:4 on page 215.

13. If you knew the exact moment of your death in advance, how would you live your life differently than you do now?

Read Psalm 39:5 on page 216.

14. In the grand scheme of things, how significant is your life?

Refer to Psalm 119:35-37 on page 217.

15. On the trip of your life, do you let God drive? Do you even let Him hold the map?

16. Where do we find meaning?

No second chances

Read pages 218-221

17. Why is it so hard for you to ask for directions?

Refer to Psalm 119:44-45 on page 218.

18. How can you really be free?

19. What does God show us in His instructions?

Prioritize your loves

Read pages 222-226.

20. Which soil are you?

21. What crop has Jesus called you to produce?

Pulling weeds

Read pages 227-230.

22. What happens to people who reject God (weeds)?

PUTTING IT ALL TOGETHER

23. In the first section (**YOU**), you reviewed your understanding of the afterlife. After reading this lesson, would you say you have a Biblical perspective? Please explain.

24. In the second section (**GOD**), you saw that God's word tells us that eternal life is a present possession, which is awarded at salvation, and must be held onto tightly. Which scripture was most relatable to you and why?

25. In the third section (***WTRMTR***), you saw that our lifetimes should be spent preparing for eternal life. Did you find a scripture that changed your perspective on Christian living? Explain.

26. This is where the rubber meets the road with God about the kind of life we should live. What will you do?

My Father in Heaven, I thank You for Your Son who died that I might have life. I can't imagine the kind of pain He suffered on the cross any more than I can imagine the anguish You felt as You watched Him die. I thank You for His victory over sin and His daily victory on our behalf. Help me to cling to this hope of eternal life, never willing to let it go, always vigilant to keep from neglecting it. I ask that You will help me see this world through Your eyes, so I'll not allow my life to be cluttered with unnecessary and meaningless things. In Your Son Jesus' Saving Name I ask all these things, Amen.

13. RULES FOR HOLY LIVING

INTRODUCTION

This lesson examines daily living.

1. What are your core values? What is your distinctive lifestyle that identifies you as a Christ-follower? What about your behavior glorifies God?

WHAT DO YOU THINK?

2. Have you ever tried to build or put something together (like a piece of furniture or a BBQ, etc.) without using the directions? How did it go?

3. Tell about a time you agonized about making a decision and eventually realized God was using that situation to give you an opportunity for real spiritual growth?

4. Did you or your family do "religious" things when you were growing up? Like what?

5. Did they bring you closer to God?

6. In your own words, what do you think the term "holy" means?

WHAT DOES GOD SAY?

God has some rules for His house, too. At first, He only had one rule for the whole world:

> *You are free to eat from any tree in the garden; but you must not eat from the tree of the knowledge of good and evil, for when you eat of it you will surely die. (Genesis 2:16–17, NIV)*

We all know how that worked out. There were only two people in the whole world back then, and they both disobeyed the one rule—and it does not matter why. Both acts of disobedience revealed something. It revealed that Eve did not trust God, and it revealed that Adam prioritized Eve above God.

7. How are you doing with your trust in God?

8. How are you doing with your priorities? Which ones are taking priority over your walk and relationship with God? (BE HONEST!)

Thousands of years later, when the nation of Israel fled Egypt, there were no rules for behavior, since the thing about the tree of the knowledge of good and evil was a moot point (no longer *could anyone* sin by eating that fruit), but God's people continued to distrust God and put things in front of Him. Given that situation, God expanded the number of rules to TEN. Here is a plain and simple version of those commandments.[1]

1. I am God, your God, who brought you out of the land of Egypt, out of a life of slavery. No other gods, only me.

2. No carved gods of any size, shape, or form of anything whatever, whether of things that fly or walk or swim. Don't bow down to them and don't serve them because I am God, your God, and I'm a most jealous God, punishing the children for any sins their parents pass on to them to the third, and yes, even to the fourth generation of those who hate me. But I'm unswervingly loyal to the thousands who love me and keep my commandments.

3. No using the name of God, your God, in curses or silly banter; God won't put up with the irreverent use of his name.

4. Observe the Sabbath day and keep it holy. Work six days and do everything you need to do. But the seventh day is a Sabbath to God, your God. Don't do any work—not you, nor your son, nor your daughter, nor your servant, nor your maid, nor your animals, not even the foreign guest visiting in your town. For in six days God made Heaven, Earth, and sea, and everything in them; he rested on the seventh day. Therefore God blessed the Sabbath day; he set it apart as a holy day.

5. Honor your father and mother so that you'll live a long time in the land that God, your God, is giving you.

6. No murder.

7. No adultery.

8. No stealing.

9. No lies about your neighbor.

10. No lusting after your neighbor's house—or wife or servant or maid or ox or donkey. Don't set your heart on anything that is your neighbor's.

---

1   Peterson, Exodus 20:2–17.

Finally Jesus, when He said it, made it super-simple: *Love God/ Love others.*

> *You shall love the Lord your God with all your heart and with all your soul and with all your mind. This is the great and first commandment. And a second is like it: You shall love your neighbor as yourself. On these two commandments depend all the Law and the Prophets. (Matthew 22:37–40, ESV)*

Nothing could be clearer, it's really very simple, but because *we are human,* nothing is harder.

9. Think about the biggest problem you are facing right now. Summarize it below. Which does it concern— loving God or loving people? (Think it through.) Depending on the analysis you ended up with, what kind of solution should you seek?

WTRMTR: HOW DOES THIS WORK IN REAL LIFE?

Some dis-assembly required

Read pages 231-233.

Jesus warned,

> *If your right eye causes you to sin, pluck it out and cast it from you; for it is more profitable for you that one of your members perish, than for your whole body to be cast into hell. And if your right hand causes you to sin, cut it off and cast it from you; for it is more profitable for you that one of your members perish, than for your whole body to be cast into hell. (Matthew 5:29–30 NKJV)*

10. What do you need to "cut out" of your life?

Refer to 1 Samuel 16:7 on page 232.

11. What does God measure when He evaluates our holiness?

12. Does this connect at all with our behavior? How?

13. What is Jack's habit regarding his goals?

14. Describe your latest "opportunity for spiritual growth."

Read Jack's story about his business on pages 233-235.

15. What did God refuse to do regarding Jack's business?

16. What did God refuse to do regarding Jack's holiness?

God's House Rules

Read pages 236-248

God has rules that *identify* what holiness is, *encourage* holy behavior, and *enable* the Christian to be holy. Some of those are given by Paul to the Colossians in Colossians 3 (on pages 236-239).

17. What did Jack identify as the secret to happiness?

18. Jack told the story of his friend Al on pages 245-246. What is your role and responsibility in holy living?

19. Why are all these rules necessary (page 247)?

PUTTING IT ALL TOGETHER

20. In the first section (**YOU**), you reviewed your previous practices. After reading this lesson, would you say that those practices had a Biblical perspective? Please explain.

21. In the second section (**GOD**), you saw the progression God's rules made, expanding and narrowing, as God's people were exposed to more of His written Word. We witnessed God's intent to make rules *simple and clear,* while our behavior tends to make things *complicated.* Which of the rule lists resonated most with you and why?

22. In the third section (**WTRMTR**), you saw some simple rules for Christian living. Almost all of them required some sort of change in character. What change would you say is the most important one for a believer to make. What change is the most important one for you to make? Explain.

23. This is where the rubber meets the road with God about our behavior. What will you do?

My Father in Heaven, I thank You that You don't conceal what You want me to do behind mysterious rituals or hidden language. Instead, Your Word tells me what I must believe and how I should behave to prove I belong to You. Thank You for being so blunt—so plain-spoken—as You have revealed Your will for me through Your Word. You keep it simple for me. You give me great beliefs and simple tasks. More than anything else, You give me Your unfailing love placed in my life through Your Son's sacrifice and resurrection. Thanks so much, Father. Help me to keep my life simple and focused on Your will by Your Holy Spirit's power. In Your Son Jesus' Name I pray these things, Amen.

14. IS LESS MORE?

INTRODUCTION

This lesson examines our call to submission and service.

1. Who's Number One? Do you expect to serve or to be served? Should we be upset when we are neglected?

WHAT DO YOU THINK?

2. Are you the leader or the follower in most of your relationships?

3. In which relationships do you lead?

4. In which relationships do you follow?

5. Does it come naturally to you to give up power and control?

6. How do you react when someone tells you what to do or not do?

7. Why do you think you act that way?

WHAT DOES GOD SAY?

New Testament servants

Jesus had high praise for the Centurion requesting healing for his servant because he recognized Christ's authority. He understood authority because he understood service. Jesus called that the greatest faith He had ever seen.

> *Jesus said to him, "I will come and heal him." The centurion answered and said, "Lord, I am not worthy that You should come under my roof. But only speak a word, and my servant will be healed. For I also am a man under authority, having soldiers under me. And I say to this one, 'Go,' and he goes; and to another, 'Come,' and he comes; and to my servant, 'Do this,' and he does it." When Jesus heard it, He marveled, and said to those who followed, "Assuredly, I say to you, I have not found such great faith, not even in Israel! ... then Jesus said to the centurion, "Go your way; and as you have believed, so let it be done for you." And his servant was healed that same hour. (Matthew 8:7–13 NKJV)*

8.	Based on this passage, what do we need to understand about the importance of authority in our lives?

Jesus planted this servant mentality in prophecy. In Isaiah 52, we see a prediction of the Messiah as the "suffering servant."

> *See, my servant will prosper; he will be highly exalted. But many were amazed when they saw him. His face was so disfigured he seemed hardly human, and from his appearance, one would scarcely know he was a man. And he will startle many nations. Kings will stand speechless in his presence. For they will see what they had not been told; they will understand what they had not heard about. (Isaiah 52:13–15, NLT)*

9.	Why did God choose to save the world using a suffering servant instead of a powerful king?

Romans 8:13-14 says,

> *For if you live according to the flesh, you will die, but if by the Spirit you put to death the deeds of the body, you will live. For all who are led by the Spirit are sons of God.*

10.	What's the importance of letting Christ take the leadership role in our lives?

11.	What are the consequences in our lives of us increasing at the expense of Christ?

WTRMTR: HOW DOES THIS WORK IN REAL LIFE?

Read pages 249-250.

12. What do you think is the *real reason* God has put you where you are?

The Forerunner

Read pages 250-251.

John the Baptist was Jesus' cousin. God sent him out to preach repentance to Israel before Jesus appeared, sort of like a political advance man. When Jesus showed up, John—who already had everybody's attention—pointed to Him and publicly announced that He was the Messiah.

Reflect on this statement from John: "He must increase and I must decrease."

13. How did John see his mission?

14. How can we be like John in attitude and actions?

15. What in your life must fade into the background so Jesus can assume His rightful position as your first priority?

Fifty/Fifty

Read pages 252-254.

16. Why is a 50/50 split with Jesus unrealistic?

17. Looking at your current circumstances, if you are being submissive to God, what does it appear that God wants for you right now?

God's Enabling = Our Responsibility

Read pages 254-257.

18. Who gets to define "abundance"? Why is that a problem for us?

19. If you don't allow Christ to increase in you, what else doesn't happen?

Beautiful Attitudes

Read pages 257-262, then refer to Matthew 5:3-10.

The *Beatitudes* are kinds of "bullet points" concerning what Christ means by "blessed."

20. What does "poor in spirit" mean? Do you believe you are "poor in spirit"?

21. How can it be a blessing to mourn just so you will be comforted?

22. On page 258, Jack shares Romans 16:1-16. What stands out about all the people Paul mentions in his closing to this letter?

23. How does the "I must decrease/He must increase" principle help us evaluate our daily service to God?

PUTTING IT ALL TOGETHER

24. In the first section (**YOU**), you considered your own attitude toward service. After reading this lesson, what do you think the main thing is that keeps you from wanting to serve? Please explain.

25. In the second section (**GOD**), you saw that scripture presents *service* as the Christian lifestyle. After reading this lesson, have you changed your mind about how your life should be going? Explain.

26. In the third section (***WTRMTR***), you saw the example of John the Baptist, whose entire purpose was to announce Christ and then fade into the background. How do feel about living life for the benefit of someone else? Is that Godly or is it pathetic? Explain.

27. This is where the rubber meets the road for obedience to God's purpose. What will you do?

My Father in Heaven, I don't like responsibility, but I love authority. Please help me to remember that YOU are the One with all the Power and Honor and Authority, and I am Your creation. I have a hard time with humility, so help me to see You as You really are. I have a hard time with obedience, so help me to notice the consequences of sinful behavior. I don't like taking the blame, so help me to understand the weight of sin and how You loved me so much, You had Your precious Son take the blame and pay the penalty for my sin so I would not be separated from you but rather together with you now and forever. More than anything, Lord, help me to be like Your Son, Who came to serve, not be served. Forgive me for my pride and arrogance. Make me one of Your servants. In Your Son Jesus' Name I pray, Amen.

15. DEAD MAN WALKING

INTRODUCTION

This lesson examines our call to die to self. Where do we draw the line in our obedience to God? What can we withhold from God? Why does God want the things we cherish?

WHAT DO YOU THINK?

Nothing counters our modern culture more than the Christian "dying to self" concept of living. Conventional wisdom is dictated by pop psychology, spoken daily on afternoon talk shows and other media and available instantly online, with experts galore telling you that your number one priority has to be getting your own needs met.

1. Does this theory match Christianity?

Self-esteem

Here is Webster's definition of self-esteem:

> 1: a confidence and satisfaction in oneself : self-respect;
>
> 2: self-conceit
>
> **Other words that have similar meaning are** ego, pridefulness, self-esteem, self-regard, self-respect. The opposite of self esteem would be defined by words like humbleness, humility, modesty[1]

2. Based on this definition, does self-esteem jibe with the personality of Jesus Christ?

3. Are you egocentric? Prideful? Humble? Modest?

WHAT DOES GOD SAY?

How does a person "die to self?" It is hard to explain the process, but we know one thing for sure: God's outstanding servants have always done it.

Shadrach, Meshach, and Abednego, like everyone else in Babylon, were ordered to worship the golden statue of the king, but they refused, even under threat of death. When given a second chance to comply with the order, they answered King Nebuchadnezzar.

> *Shadrach, Meshach and Abednego replied to him, "King Nebuchadnezzar, we do not need to defend ourselves before you in this matter. If we are thrown into the blazing furnace, the God we serve is able to deliver us from it, and he will deliver us from Your Majesty's hand. But even if he does not, we want you to know, Your Majesty, that we will not serve your gods or worship the image of gold you have set up." (Daniel 3:16–18 NIV)*

4. Where is your line in the sand? How stubborn are you willing to be for God?

---

1   http://www.merriam-webster.com/dictionary/self-esteem

> *Queen Esther was the only person with a remote chance to stop the genocide of the Jews by the Persians, and it was far from certain that she would even have a chance to intervene, since no one could come into the king's presence without the king's summoning—including the queen. Calling upon the king without permission was a capital offence, punishable by death, but Esther fasted and prayed and set her mind to try: "I will go to the king, even though it is against the law. And if I perish, I perish." (Esther 4:16, NIV)*

5. When it comes to serving Christ, what is your position? "There's nothing I can do," or "There's nothing I won't do." Can you prove that? Where's your evidence?

> *Jesus insisted that His disciples simply cannot hold onto the things of this world or put anything ahead of God, because that is a sure way to lose life—both temporal and eternal: "The man who loves his life will lose it, while the man who hates his life in this world will keep it for eternal life." (John 12:25, NIV)*

6. What do you think about self-preservation being the first natural law after hearing that?

7. What specific things in your life should be put to death?

8. What in your life is important enough for you to hold onto instead of Jesus?

WTRMTR: HOW DOES THIS WORK IN REAL LIFE?

Verdict

Read Jack's story on pages 263-264.

9. What does it take to be "God's guy"?

10. What does it mean to "live for self"?

Who do I have to kill?

Read page 265.

11. Why did Hawk have to be killed?

12. What does it mean to "die to self"?

Death sentence

Read pages 266-269, and refer to 1 Peter 2:24 on page 266.

13. What did Christ accomplish that enables us to die to sin?

Refer to Romans 14:7-8 on page 266.

14. What did Paul receive in return for dying to sin?

Refer to Galatians 2:20-21 on page 267.

15. What did Paul have that was crucified with Christ on the cross?

16. How does your life plan differ from God's life plan for you?

Chain of Custody

Read pages 270-279.

17. With what do you absolutely trust God?

18. With what are you hesitant to trust God?

19. With what do you absolutely not trust God?

Refer to Galatians 1:3-5 on page 272.

20. Why were you created?

21. React to Johnny Hunt's quote: "We have all eternity to enjoy our victories, but only one lifetime to earn them."

22. Look at the "situation," as Jack breaks it down on page 278. In light of that, how would you evaluate a decision to refuse to die to sin?

PUTTING IT ALL TOGETHER

23. In the first section (**YOU**), you looked at the basic human needs as dictated by "self-esteem." After reading this lesson, do you see how those needs can keep people from dying to sin? Please explain.

24. In the second section (**GOD**), you saw scripture example of people who were willing to die completely to sin—and die physically in the process. After reading this lesson, do you think those people were realistic? Please explain.

25. In the third section (***WTRMTR***), you saw that the determining factor for dying to self is trusting God. Do you have experience with this struggle? Describe your struggle and how it's going.

26. Dying to sin is where the rubber meets the road for living to God. What will you do?

My Father in Heaven, as I conclude this series of lessons, I know that You have spoken to me from Your Word and the experience and wisdom of others. You have even spoken to me from my own experience and imagination. I thank you for this final word. I pray, Lord, that You will teach me to come to You, bow to Your will, and die to my sin. No retreat, no surrender, no regrets, no looking back. Thank You, Lord, for saving my soul. Thank You, Lord, for making me whole. Thank You, Lord, for my salvation, my life, the certainty of my place in Heaven, and for filling me with your peace and joy. Truly the greatest blessing I've ever received. In Jesus' Name I pray, Amen.